THE STREETS OF LIVERPOOL

A PHOTOGRAPHIC RECORD COMPILED BY COLIN WILKINSON

Front cover: The Black Bull, Walton, 1926. Hand colouring by Peter Turner
Back cover: Steble Fountain, c.1895 (C.F. Inston)

Published in 1993 by: The Bluecoat Press,
                      Bluecoat Chambers,
                      Liverpool
                      (051-707 2390)

Photographic credits: The Photographs are reproduced courtesy of the City Engineer,
Liverpool City Council, with the following exceptions:
Bluecoat Press (41), Royal Commission for Historical Monuments (24),
Elsam, Mann and Cooper (15, 21), National Museums and Galleries on
Merseyside (10), Karl Hughes (62), Michael Day (13,36), Harry Major (11),

Typesetting: Typebase Limited
Printed by: Printeksa

ISBN 1 872568 07 6

THE STREETS OF LIVERPOOL

A PHOTOGRAPHIC RECORD COMPILED BY COLIN WILKINSON

The Bluecoat Press

Introduction

In July, 1845, the Prince Consort opened a new dock in Liverpool and in doing so, bestowed royal approval on the ambitious and forward looking business community. The Albert Dock was a commercial venture on the grand scale; a response to the needs for secure and fireproof warehousing to cope with the massive flow of trade into the port. Herman Melville, author of 'Moby Dick' was one of many visitors who compared the miles of docks along the river with the Great Wall of China and the Pyramids of Egypt; so unprecedented was the scale of trade, it was hardly surprising that the port was seen in such comparative terms as a modern wonder of the world.

Liverpool was exploding. The demands of trade created, in their turn, a demand for labour and the hopeful flocked to the city seeking opportunities denied elsewhere. For some, their optimism was rewarded and wealth was created on a staggering scale. Tony Lane, in 'Liverpool: Gateway of Empire', asserts that, "London apart, Liverpool produced more wealthy families than any other English city. At its peak, in the years 1890-1899, Liverpool produced as many millionaires as Greater Manchester, West Yorkshire, West Midlands, Tyneside and East Anglia combined." Major companies prospered in a time of unbridled capitalism and the Corporation engaged itself in erecting monuments to its prosperity and international status. St. George's Hall stands as an eloquent symbol of the ambitions of a town that was challenging London as the commercial centre of the British Empire.

Ironically, in 1847, the year that the young architect of St. George's Hall, Harvey Lonsdale Elmes died, aged 33, over 300,000 poor Irish landed in the port. Escaping famine in their own country, they must have been astonished by the magnificent building nearing completion on the plateau perched above the docks and town centre. No doubt, many immigrants felt they had, indeed, arrived in a town where the streets were paved with gold but the busy quays, elegant public buildings and fine merchants' houses were hiding a grimmer reality from which few would escape. Housing conditions were already appalling, with thousands crammed into cellars and filthy, insanitary courts. The 1842 Report on the Sanitary Conditions of the Labouring Population spoke out against the horrors it found. 'More filth, worse physical suffering and moral disorder than Howard describes as affecting the prisons, are to be found among the cellar population of the working people of Liverpool.' The continued influx of impoverished families made it virtually impossible for the town to respond unaided. The consequences have been well documented with horrific epidemics regularly sweeping through the packed slums that were being rapidly erected around the town centre.

The need for action was not generally accepted by the ruling classes. There was a pervading attitude that poverty would always be a corollary of prosperity but the consequences of over-crowding were increasingly too close for comfort. The pioneering work of Doctor Duncan was instrumental in creating wider awareness of the root causes of epidemics and helped galvanise a somewhat lethargic Corporation. Duncan, along with other public health reformers, saw an obvious link between housing and environmental conditions and the incidence of frequent outbreaks of cholera, smallpox and typhus. Sir John Simon, London's first medical officer of health, succinctly pinpointed the cause of such ravages of the population as 'the foul air and foul water of undrained, unpaved, unscavenged, unwashed, unlighted, unventilated localities and housing.' Worried by constant oubreaks of cholera, in particular, the Corporation appointed Duncan to be the first Medical Officer of Health in the country, appropriately coinciding with a major outbreak of typhus fever in the wake of the wave of Irish immigration that year (1847). In Duncan's first year of office, over 21,000 people died, one in fifteen of the population. Mass burials were regular occurrences; in 1849, 572 deaths were notified in one August week alone. Outbreaks of measles, scarlatina and diptheria added to the heavy death toll, particularly amongst children. In 1861, there were 12,900 infant deaths, 6,500 were children under five.

By 1870, the work of Duncan was having some effect, although the problems of overcrowding were still chronic. William Farr, a statistician, claimed that the population of Liverpool was 66,000 to the square mile, an incredible population density of one person for every seven square yards. A City Engineer's report in 1864 had listed 18,500 insanitary houses and over 3,000 congested courts but the continuing expansion of the population and the demands for cheap accommodation thwarted any major plans to reverse the tide of insanitary housing. The building of St. Martin's Cottages, in 1869, was the first major initiative, representing possibly the earliest municipal housing in the country but it was an isolated effort and barely touched the overall problem. However, the principle of municipal involvement had been set and new initiatives gathered momentum. The building of tenement blocks maintained Liverpool's pioneering reputation and, under the inspired leadership of City Engineer John Brodie, new materials were introduced to speed up the building process. His use of prefabricated, reinforced concrete in Eldon Street (photograph, p.29), represented a technical breakthrough that was rapidly taken up worldwide. The Liver Building, built three years later, shows how rapidly the new technology was accepted.

The years up to the Second World War witnessed a massive expansion of municipal housing. The progressive designs of City Architect, Sir Lancelot Keay, were instrumental in raising standards. For many, houses with running water and internal toilet facilities became a reality for the first time. Thousands of families, however, continued to suffer from the Victorian legacy, a burden that refused to go away and at times, even worsened, particularly in the 1930's economic depression.

It is this legacy that can be seen so dramatically in the photographs in Part Two. It is difficult to imagine a greater contrast between the prosperity of a major world port and the poverty of most of its inhabitants. The photographs in Part One are of a confident city, bustling with trade and prosperity. Lord Street, Church Street and Dale Street are thronged with people and traffic. The names of the shops such as Bon Marché (p.7) and the Japanese Tea Rooms (p.12) project a cosmopolitan outlook that is in keeping with the city's trading importance but the affluence of the city centre hides another world. Who could guess from looking at Bunney's emporium (p.13) that scarcely one mile away, on Brownlow Hill, the Workhouse was accommodating a population of some 5,000 souls; a town within a town. In 1884, an observer had written about 'hordes of the ragged and the wretched men and women in the cruellest grip of poverty, little children with shoeless feet, bodies pinched' while 'the superb carriages of the rich, with their freights of refined and elegant ladies threaded their way among sections of the population so squalid and miserable my heart ached for them.'

Charles Dickens had a great love of Liverpool and even enrolled as a special constable to seek out characters and atmosphere for his novels. It was tempting to call this book 'A Tale of Two Cities', since the contrast between poverty and prosperity exposed in these photographs is more in keeping with such a title than a romantic tale of the French Revolution but even Charles Dickens would have been shocked to see such conditions perpetuated a century after he had exposed the disgrace of poverty and the slums in 'Oliver Twist'.

Looking at some of the photographs taken nearly a century later, it is difficult to imagine the lives many people have lived in the shadow of the great wealth of the city. The photographs record a past that must still provoke fierce memories, for many of the children recorded in the streets and closes will now be drawing their pensions and, perhaps, reflecting with mixed feelings on the city they grew up in.

THE PHOTOGRAPHS

Most of the photographs in this book are taken from a unique collection held by the City Engineer's Department. Many were originally printed in an earlier version of 'The Streets of Liverpool' but in this revised and extended edition, new photographs have been added to give a broader picture of the city, especially of the waterfront.

The City Engineer began commissioning photographs in 1897 to document aspects of his department's activities. One of the earliest surviving photographs (number 6 in their files) and probably taken to illustrate poor housing conditions, is the stark image of Emily Place reproduced on page 40.

Many of the photographs in the collection are less poignant, documenting everyday work such as road improvements, refuse collection and laying sewers. There is extensive documentation of major projects including the infilling of George's Dock to build the Liver Building (page 14), the reclamation of land to construct Otterspool Promenade and the expansion of the road network out of the city centre. Traffic surveys often resulted in fascinating street photographs, including the city centre scenes reproduced on pages 26-32. The city centre photographs record a bustling and affluent city with impressive shops, grand public buildings and streets thronged with well-dressed workers and shoppers. Only occasionally does the sight of another world intrude, as in the photograph of a shawled woman carrying her baby in Lime Street (page 33). For the other side of Liverpool, we have to turn to the second part of the book, to the photographs taken to illustrate poor housing conditions and chronic overcrowding.

There can be few collections that so comprehensively capture the scale of urban poverty. A particular quality of the photographs is that they were taken simply as everyday working documents. There was no underlying social or political motivation involved, the photographer was just carrying out the requirements of his job. The children and adults captured in every scene were rarely posed by the photographer; they formed impromptu groups in response to what must have been a novel experience, for few photographers cared to venture down the backstreets without good reason.

In contrast, the photograph of childen carrying bottles of beer in Burlington Street (page 41) was taken specifically for temperance work by the photographer N. Stephen and was one of a series shown regularly at Band of Hope meetings to warn of the effects of the 'demon drink'.

Using a hidden camera to avoid detection, Stephen produced photographs which, whilst lacking the clarity of the carefully taken City Engineer's photographs, manage to record the depths of hopelessness and despair of slum living.

The use of such photographs, especially lantern slides, were particularly popular at that time. The commentary to one set of lantern slides produced by the Temperance Society in 1892 reveals an interesting assessment of cause and effect:

'Hardly a day passes which does not, through the medium of Police Courts or Coroner's Court, bring shocking evidence to light of the poverty, squalor and depravity that abounds in the midst of wealth and prosperity.... it is generally admitted that drunkeness is the source of the largest proportion of poverty, of vice, of crime, of poorly-clad and ill-fed children.'

The real nature of life in the slums is well-hidden; the photographs giving only an impression of the lives many people endured. However, without them, our knowledge of working-class life is diminished. Photography captures changing dress, transport, buildings and life styles in a way no other medium can and the City Engineer's collection is a vital record of life in Liverpool in the twentieth century. Fortunately, the photographic department continues to document the transformation of the city. These photographs will, in turn, become the historical documents of the future.

THE CITY CENTRE

GEORGE'S DOCK, c.1885

SALTHOUSE DOCK, 1897

AQUITANIA AT THE LANDING STAGE, c.1920

THE LANDING STAGE, 1899

THE LANDING STAGE, 1925

CANNING DOCK, 1911

INFILLING GEORGE'S DOCK, 1907

PIER HEAD, 1947

PIER HEAD SHELTER, 1902

MANN ISLAND, c.1895

NEW QUAY, 1908

GOREE PIAZZAS, 1913

WATER STREET STATION, LIVERPOOL OVERHEAD RAILWAY, 1910

LIVERPOOL OVERHEAD RAILWAY, 1956

SOUTH CASTLE STREET, 1907

ST GEORGE'S CRESCENT, 1900

BON MARCHÉ, CHURCH STREET, 1891

BON MARCHÉ, 1900

LORD STREET, 1908

CORNER OF LORD STREET AND WHITECHAPEL, 1908

CHURCH STREET, 1908

CORNER OF WHITECHAPEL, 1908

NORTH JOHN STREET, 1908

DALE STREET, 1908

HOUGHTON STREET, 1908

LIME STREET, 1913

QUEEN SQUARE, 1920

ST JOHN'S MARKET, 1909

CASTLE STREET AND THE TOWN HALL, c.1900

ST GEORGE'S HALL, 1906

ST PETER'S CHURCH, 1908

*'Separate territories assigned to poverty.
Removed from the sight of happier classes,
poverty may struggle along as it can.'*

Friedrich Engels (1844)

EMILY PLACE, 1897

BURLINGTON STREET, 1893

ELDON STREET, 1910

ELDON STREET, 1905

ROAD SWEEPERS, HUNTER STREET, 1916

SCOTLAND ROAD, 1908

CARTWRIGHT PLACE, 1926

BURLINGTON STREET, 1934

CHILDWALL STREET, 1909

NETHERFIELD ROAD, 1927

HUNTER STREET, 1927

CLARE STREET, 1927

GEORGE'S HILL, 1927

GERRARD STREET, 1927

KEMPSTON STREET, 1933

POWNALL SQUARE, 1906

TICHBOURNE TERRACE, 1935

JOHNSON STREET, 1935

SILVESTER STREET, 1934

BANCROFT STREET, 1934

LAWRENCE STREET, 1935

READING STREET, 1956

HAVELOCK STREET, 1960

EVERTON BROW, 1927